4play

Kristie LeVangie

iUniverse, Inc.
Bloomington

4play

iUniverse books may be ordered through booksellers or by contacting:

iUniverse
1663 Liberty Drive
Bloomington, IN 47403
www.iuniverse.com
1-800-Authors (1-800-288-4677)

ISBN: 978-1-4697-9838-7 (sc)
ISBN: 978-1-4697-9839-4 (ebk)

Printed in the United States of America

iUniverse rev. date: 03/13/2012

This book is dedicated to the playmakers and the dream chasers.

4WORD

Fifty years ago in his unique and distinguishable voice, Bob Dylan gave us the line, "The times, they are a'changin'." It was true then, and it continues to be true today. Our society is changing before our very eyes. Gone are the days when men "brought home the bacon", and women were expected to "fry it up in the pan." Women are wielding more power, and we are in the midst of gender role transference. The same can be seen in the sex industry.

Thanks in many ways to advanced technologies, each of our desires and fantasies are only a mouse click away. We no longer have to be part of an inner circle, seeking out secret clubs to indulge our sexual desires. We no longer have to keep our fantasies a secret for fear of what society may think of us. We can cater to our desires from the privacy of our homes, and once we start the adventure, we soon find out, that regardless of our tastes, we are not alone, and some can seem a bit darker than others.

We are no longer a society that is keeping our sexuality hidden behind bedroom doors. We are talking about it, and we are advertising it. We are taking control of it and finding ways to improve it. But perhaps because we are still a tactile-craved species, regardless of the advancements in technologies, we are branching outside of our PCs, laptops, and tablets. We are still seeking the good old-fashioned book; where we can highlight our favorite lines, make notes in the margins, and dog-ear our favorite pages.

For decades, the "sex industry" has been limited to adult stores, clubs, and magazines. I don't think I over-exaggerate when I say much of the industry has catered to the man, even though the woman has proven to be just as much a sexually-driven creature. Thanks to sociologists and neuroscientists working together, we are learning more and more about the brain and what it is we find sexually stimulating, (i.e., what turns us on and why).

Being the social scientist in mind and the writer at heart, K—is even more. She is a movement. She is helping pave the way for women to be seen as forces and not simply objects of desire.

*With her first book, **Libidacoria: In a Plain Brown Wrapper,** she shocked us into reality with her harsh words and seduced us with her graphic details. She continues this reality in **4play**. She proves that women think, say, feel, and do "dirty" things. She shows the emotion that at times empowers us, and simultaneously, often makes us victims of ourselves. She, like all women, is truly a "lady of colors."*

This is not a book just for women. As with all K—'s writings, men will get sucked in as well. They will get lost in the fantasies of her experiences and desires, and find themselves wishing to be on the receiving end of everything she has to offer.

Regardless of your gender, these poems will draw you in and teach you. You will be able to relate to at least one of these poems, and if you can't relate, you'll want to. K—puts on these pages what most of us have felt but have been too afraid to admit. Women who read these pages won't be able to help but feel more empowered and driven. Men are being given the chance to peer into the mind of a woman and learn that we are not always what your mama may have told you we were.

*K—'s poetry is like everyone's sexuality . . . a portal into a higher realm. Use her experiences as a key for your own inspiration, your own **4play**.*

Katrina "Saxie" Buckley
Co-host of
Libidacoria: The Late Night Talk Show

I'm the girl they like to abuse.
To fuck,
To suck,
To batter and use.

I do it to myself
By allowing the sleaze.
Part of the addiction,
The torturous disease.

I'll never be more
Than I allow myself to.
I fucked it all up
At every turn.

A lifetime commitment
To the crash
And the burn.

My mother raised a whore.
Not that it was her fault, mind you.
I was just born this way—
Ready
And willing to play—

House
Or doctor . . .
Even innocent games
Turned into scavenger hunts
Through adolescent bodies.

I yearn for the touch . . .
At the point
It becomes too much,
And I cross the line
Between reality
And desire.

It's in **that** moment
That my soul is fed,
And all my troubles
Are laid to bed.

When my desire to live
Overtakes my desire to die,
And outward pleasure
Is desperately sealed inside.

It's the moment when
I become whole,
And you
Realize you are incomplete

In a place without deceit,
Where you and I meet,
Face-to-face . . .

Or sometimes
Face-to-genitalia.

It's a place so intimate,
Words are never needed,
Expectations are superseded,
And our purpose is stated . . .

But you, like I,
Will never be sated.

It's the nature of the profession.

It's the seed of the obsession.

And I stand before you infected.

Come in from the rain.
Come in from the rain.

Grab a towel
And a warm hole.

Make yourself at home
For a little while.

Scratch your name
Into my brain
And kiss me
Taking my breath away.

Now stay.

Now stay.

Now . . .
Stay . . . .

Now go,
. . . But back off slow
And allow for me
To catch you.

Now insert the slot,
Release what you got,
And scream my name
In the morning!

Come in from the rain.
That's your warning.

Sensuality comes to me
Quicker than other girls,
Slicker than other girls,
Sicker than other girls.

It's that intensity
That runs most men off
And their inexperience
That scares them away.

I didn't ask to be this way!

I didn't ask to be
Overwhelming,
Touching, smelling,
Feeling and feeling
And feeling
And feeling . . .

I just didn't ask.

And now I
Have the task
Of suppressing?

Digressing?

Not obsessing?

Experience is my aphrodisiac,
My addiction,
My mental affliction.

They love to put on a good show,
But under,
Below,
They're fretting the next move.
. . . And I'm just . . .
Being.

If they could stop deciding to live
And just live,
They might find
The sensuality
A challenge they could keep up with.

With him,
I like to embrace my pain.
It's the delightful punishment
He puts in my brain.
Or is it a reward?
To be used and then thrown?
Come, bury the bone.
Come, bury the bone.

The edge of his teeth,
The slapping reprieve,
The piercing brutality
Of his final release.
With me, he can do anything that he please.
I'm here on my knees.
I'm here on my knees.

I'm reminded with fingertips
Over delicately-bruised skin,
To let it all in . . .
To let it all in . . .

Here we go again,
I've forsaken love for sin.
A battle I never win,
But always overcome.

I play dumb
Pretending never to see,
But there's always insecurity—

Wrapped in weed,
Wrapped in speed,
Wrapped in sex.

Simplistic and complex.

I am a "However" girl,
A Nothing-Better-to-do-with-my-Time girl,
A substitution for a greater desire.
And like a piece of art
With no proper showcase,
My value depreciates
With each broken heart,
Each "Just Not Quite Right" outcome.
If I could learn
To give up hope for anything more,
Expect the unexpected
Not-Quite-Happy ending,
And let go
Of the notion of probability,
I think I could enjoy
The lack of meaning I have
And resolve
To never be more.

I steal away with him
In graphic display
Of illusion.

I pretend his words
Carry weight
Not motive.

He pretends to want
What he can
Never have.

And both of us
Become partially
Fulfilled.

I want to feel
Complete emersion,
Spontaneous combustion,
And hypnotic euphoria.

I want your hands
On me,
Around me,
Inside me . . .

I want your tongue
Slick,
And with words
That read
From a bathroom wall.

I want your power,
But I want you
To fight for it.
Willing to give up
Just in the right moment.

I want your Being
Extracted,
Hips active,

And groveling at my feet.

I want to tear more from you
Than just your clothes . . .
Through verse and prose.

You come to me like a tickle.
A thousand hairs stand on end
When you begin.

There's magic in that space
Right before we touch . . .

Almost too much.

I long to end
Before you even begin.

Like magnets of similar poles,
We push and pull apart
And movement becomes art.
Synchronized in fluid ballet.

And yet we stay,
Close to the edge,
Looking over.
Both of us wanting to dive
Off the cliff,
But not wanting to
More.

Push and pull,
Until we're full,
Overwhelmed by nature
And nurture.
Fully sure
Of our own intentions . . .

And divine intervention
Pushes us,
With one finger,
Over . . .

And gravity
Pulls us down
To bliss . . .
To this.

I'm never more close to Heaven,
Than with eyes closed,
An arched pose,
And your finger gently touching.

It's in this suspension
Of tortured affliction,
My desire for friction,
My hunger for addiction . . .
That I could lose myself.

An hour,
A day,
A fortnight of play . . .

Here's where I'd stay . . .

Alive,
Unsatisfied,
Electrified
And wanting.

You are my desire,
A flesh-burning fire.
And I,
Am your
Object inflamed.

She wore her sensuality like a cloak.
Gracefully dancing between men,
Inviting sin,
But never more.
She only loved to explore.
To dig to their core,
But she would never let them in.
She wore too many masks,
And buried the very essence of her being.

You look better to me
At night
In dimmed light
And semi-romantic intention,
Than in the day
When survival
Pulls you away.

If I can capture
A random thought,
A fleeting moment,
An elicit response . . .

If I can learn trust,
Mix friendship and lust,
And stop looking at the clock . . .

I might learn to recognize you
In the daylight.

Lady black
With lips full red,
Bosom lifted,
Appendages spread.

Lady red,
Passions pure black,
Desire tempting
With every attack.

Lady blue,
Tissue in hand,
Eyes swollen,
Sitting in sand.

Lady pink
With full spring skirt,
Designer heels,
Smiles away the hurt.

Lady white,
Charitable belle,
Heart now golden
From personal hell.

Lady green,
Scruples in-tact,
Whore for money
She lays on her back.

Lady gray,
Never absolute,
Perfectly balanced,
Ideas to pollute.

Lady clear,
Transparently ill,
Lies to herself
She's colorful still.

Standing in the tub,
You
T
O
W
E
R above
My sexuality and my imagination.

Water pouring D
                 O
                    W
                       N,

I listen to the sound.

My heart beating
In anticipation.

I drink your libation,
Creating sensation,
And a stir
I do
Not
Want
To stop.

Here, I'm caught.

Wanting
The very essence
Of you.

There's pot under my fingernails.
There's cocaine on my lips.
Ecstasy courses through my blood.
Viagra in my hips.

My pain cries for the morphine.
My mania for crystal meth,
Rambunctiousness for Ritalin,
Nicotine in every breath.

My diet, shooting heroine.
Mental health, acid provides.
LSD, for my clarity,
And opium where I reside.

Those lips that I traced,
Your hands on my waist
As we sat on the living room sofa.

That look in your eye,
That lack of surprise,
Tells me exactly what it's about.

That cock that I seized,
Slowly teased,
And then pleased,
Is thinking about it now.

Isn't he?

Tied
> I cannot see

Bound
> Cannot move arms or feet

And gagged
> Cannot speak

Frozen
> With anticipation

Paralyzed
> With excitement

Scared
> Of your sadism

Longing
> To be hit

Wanting
> To be raped

Desire
> To be taken

When
> Your passion exceeds your self-control

Where
> Desire exceeds your conservatism

Why
> Because you can

What
> Take me

How

Suspended
Somewhere between
Pleasure   and   Anticipation.

Turn me on
With speedometer
Racing the clock.

I'm a seedy
Odometer
Sucking your cock.

It's the exquisite mastery
You'll recall
When I'm gone.

It's how all the others
Are desperate yawns.

You're no closer to Heaven
Than when I am filled,
A twisted fate you so
Consciously sealed.
The day you opened
The entrance to Hell
With a cloaked little girl
And her rebel yell.

With lights down low
And bedroom door closed,
I'm a succubus
In garter and hose.

And the movements are
Slow . . .

As I start from below
And work my way
Up to your soul.

I am more than a hole.

I am everything
You've ever known.

We defy tradition,
A conscious, deliberate decision.
We fuck
With some conditions.

You never make promises
We both know
That you will never keep.

You never bear emotion,
Outside of selfish lust
And never lift the veil
Of mystery and mistrust.

If I cry out for you,
You'll ignore my aching need,

And I will drop everything
The moment you text
To be where you want me to be.

There!

Inside me . . .

You'll turn on the lies,
The truth-hiding and—bending
Until I have to kiss you
To shut you up.

It's cute that you lie
And don't think that I
Know you are doing it.

Once unclothed,
You no longer see me
Overwhelmed by your desire for me,
And I no longer matter.

And once your cock has played,
You rush away.
I imagine in disgust,
Of what I've become
To be with you.

Make me feel you.
Make me fire.
Masculate yourself
In my desire.

Come at me.
Indulge me in pain.
Take from me
Until nothing remains.

Mouth, tongue,
Finger, cock.
Lick, suck,
Finger, fuck.

Make me hate you.
Make me scream.
Force me further,
Set the scene.

Tease me wickedly
Sparing none.
My protesting
Is half the fun.

I say to you come with me.
Down into the dark,
Where sense of sight is overshadowed,
Overpowered by touch.
Let me explore you
In the depths that you'll allow.
Close your eyes.
You don't need them now.
I'll nibble and claw,
Swallow and paw
Until your desire overwhelms you.
Once there,
Extremities swelled,
Flood me
In your Knowing.

I concede to you
And your parade.
Peacock feathers spread
Over your head
Trying to get my attention.

Do you feel the tension?

I try to bat you away
But your persistence
Wears down my resistance.
I'm looking for substance
Inside the pretty package.

Are you up for that presentation?

That will require some thought.
And you figured
I might have bought
The whole
Without seeing its parts.

That presumption
Dubs you.
I'm not looking to get fucked.

Anything more
That you have tucked
In that pretty little head of yours?

I lay there with him
Thinking of you.
Myself wasted
In another moment
Of selfish want.

And thoughts enter me
Of you entering me
On that hot, dark night.

You live more in my imagination
Than out of it.
But our time will come.
And I will soon
Lay with you
On that hot, dark night.

I close my eyes,
Begin to explore my body
Imagining you exploring
For the first time.
I grow warmer
And you could not be nearer
Unless you were nearer
On that hot, dark night.

I struggle to remain still,
Remain quiet.
Aware that this is for you,
Not for him.
There is nothing for him
Beyond what he got last night.
And when he leaves my door,
He will never return
On a hot, dark night.

You, however,
Have me.
Bits of my day
Given to you,
Lost in thought.
The only one to hold power over me.
The only one I will allow to,
For this, I release all that is in me
For you
On this hot, dark night.

I ache with need,
Weight of a man,
Weak in the knees,
None of it planned.
The groping of bodies,
The moanings of lust,
Definitions of naughty,
Thrust after thrust.
The internal struggle
Between greed and desire,
Fueling the ego,
Fueling the fire.
Capturing that moment,
Where you lose yourself
In finding me.

How much more tempting
Could it be?

His belt buckle
On my nightstand
Tells the tale
Of nights in abandon
And once shattered hope.
His rebirth,
His re-emergence . . .
Our rebirth
Fills me to the rim
With sin
And innocence.
He has me almost convinced
To give myself.
When he's gone,
The feeling's wrong.
It's empty.
It's sad.
It's quiet.
And I hate
That I hate it so much.
But it's all erased
With his touch.

I wonder how I found myself here
In a world so full
Of endless possibility.
At times, my senses overload.

I find eroticism
In everything around me.

Tonight,
The air is electric.
An urgency cries
For much needed attention.

An ionic catapult itches me,
Stripped to my core.
Exposing vulnerability.

It's in this place
Where the unknown
Feels surreal . . .
But feels so fucking real.

I bite my lip to take it all in,
To breathe it all in,
To invite it all in.
The exquisite consumption of sin.

He came on my ass,
His cock made of glass,
Slick,
Hard,
Unforgiving,
Unrelenting . . .

That desperate need
Between fulfillment
And greed
Where thought takes
A backseat to libido.

He read my skin,
My letting him in,
My desire
And my credo.

There is sin in his lips,
Dominance in his hips,
And euphoria
In his fingertips.

That brought me to this,
His entrancing kiss
And proof of his desire
On my backside.

Come.
Let me bend before you.
Let me offer
Warmth,
Slick, wet comfort,
And awakening.
Let me summon
Your manhood
Through tense muscles
And harshly spoken moans.

Let me devour
The shower
Of your addiction,
Your obsession
With the transgression

That has me
Bending before you.

Come.
Let me offer before you.

Let me bend
Realities,
Fantasies,
And harshly spoken moans.

Enter me
Like a demon
With one aim—
To penetrate my soul.

Stuff me.
Stab me.
Fill me with your cock.

Impale me
By your passion.

I want to feel
You want me.

I want to be opened,
Entered,
And sated.

Pierce me fiercely,
And when climax comes,
Deposit within me
Your desire,
Evidence of our fire,
And lay there just a minute
So that I might capture
The moment.

Six hands,
Thirty toes,
Two penises
And a juicy cunt.
Full of curiosity
And craving
And want.

Sensory hyper drive,
Ocean of lust,
Licking,
Grasping,
Feeling
Each thrust.

Intoxicated by taboo,
By nervous greed,
By strange sensation,
And transcendent need.

Two hands,
Ten toes,
Hard nipples,
Wet cunt,
And desire
To consume
As much
As I want.

We came together,
Broken,
Few words spoken,
And fucked like animals in heat.

I suffered your lies,
False alibis,
Misery and deceit.

I pretended
To not be offended
And smiled
Until I cried.

Those eyes that catch me—
Somewhere between,
Ecstasy and release.
The twinkle is the tease,
The raised eyebrow—
The disease,
And the intensity
Brings me to my knees.

It's in these
I find comfort
To express myself
In all my desire.

You
Can handle my fire.

It's there
In those eyes.

This terror sits within my gut,
Where the virgin overtakes the slut
And hope hangs on by a tiny,
Miniscule
Remnant
Of thread.

It's time like these
I'd rather be dead . . .

Or disintegrate into thin air instead.

To digest a world
Where you can't exist,
Because the heart aches
With such brutal force

That it rips my insides
Into pieces like this . . .
And from reality
I must divorce.

To you,
I am merely meat,
A psychologist
To your cock-enabled seat,
And a place
Of lurid retreat.

Death has never seemed so sweet.

Points in the day
When I feel release.
The pressure created
When entering me.

The tighter hole
Of scandalous delight.
A dirty whore
Bit pillows last night.

Relaxation
Let you in
To the sanctity
Of anal sin.

Slow to begin . . .

Slow to begin . . .

In vaginal slop,
The juices drop
And lubricate
The action.

Both enhancement
And distraction

From tightly
Restricted
Injection.

I feel you grow.

Body jolting,
Morals revolting
In repulsive display
Of your cock
In my backside
For sadistic play.

The wider you grown,
The longer you grow,
I must reciprocate
By allowing you to.

I find a place
Where I relax
Into the pain,

Where your pleasure
Dominates
Without restrain.

And I lose myself here
While finding myself.

Life liven
In chunks of figure eights.
Self-destructing masterpiece
Right out of the gates.

A self-created,
Full masturbated,
Recyclable hell.

Two on, two off,
Half in, half out,
Plié, Penchée,
Spinning around.

I make myself sick
In the movement,

Crescendoing to ends
That never begin
How I want them to
And never finish on time.

Waiting for a sign
That never comes,
I reason that I'm dumb,

But I know . . .
It's the come's and go's
In the show

Waiting for the dress rehearsal to end.

Close the curtains,
Clean the theater,
Again tomorrow,
Price is steeper.

I'm never more alive
Than when you're with me,
In thought . . .
In bed . . .

Inebriated in desire,
You mix like toxin
In my head.

I'm uplifted,
Sifted,
And stapled together
With pieces you left behind.

You exist within
The residue of my mind
Coming to light,
The very moment
I decide to forget you.

I never love myself as much
As the moment I cum
At my own touch.

Pleasures come by my own hand,
And filthy thoughts
You can't understand.

There's darkness and bleeding,
A welcoming ache,
That deepens to pleasure
For fucking fuck's sake.

#1

I can't tell you what to do.
I can only assure
You'll suffer no more.
But you must choose me.

I lack creativity,
Hubris,
And vice.
. . . But the view is nice.

Church on Sunday,
Family picnics,
And a beautiful Lexus.

Attentive in the bedroom
Worship on my knees.
My aim—to please.

But if you expect to be taken,
It can't happen.
I care too much
To hurt you.

Malleable
And flimsy,
My desire, your whimsy.

My crimson is yours
To bleed out
Over evenings ending in bubbles
And tender surrender.

#2

I can tell you what to do.
It's what I do.
And you will ache and suffer
Because you want to.

I am conceit,
Deceit,
Friction . . .
Your seething addiction.

Pool in lodges,
Grab-ass in smoky bars,
And Saturday morning cartoons.

Demanding and forceful display.
There's where you lay

And I'll use you to get off.
Like a little girl
I long to break.

I will begin gentle,
Then overshadowed by my desire,
Breathe heavy with fire
Into your vagina.

I am rock
For you to chip away at for years
Convincing yourself there is molten core.

Would you ever want more?

He plagues me like an addiction.
A cold turkey withdrawal
With hot flash flashbacks.
Bright bulb visions of
Clothes strewn about the floor,
Hands grasping sheets,
Words burning the ears,
And heat overtaking my thighs.

All his lies, All his lies,
I snorted like cocaine
Sliced razor-fine on a mirror.

And I wonder how I got back here—

Veins bulging,
Track marks bleeding,
Pulse racing,
Addiction aching

. . . And all he did was wave.

I calculate equations
Of your actions
Plus my reactions,
Multiplied by my paranoia,
And fucked up historical design.

I use every mathematical sign
To make sense of this.

I subtract my perceptions
In hopes to see
If this is less than sadistic,
Greater than optimistic
And equal to a tangent
I've never taken before.

Unfulfilled with
Lips so sealed,
That I envy
My own devices.

It's always like this
In crisis—

When transformation
Makes you feel deranged,
Though nothing yet has changed,
Everybody's fucked up
And on stage.

A real moment
Is the new elusive hunt.
It's no longer my cunt.

I bounce in misdirection
Toward my final goal,

But this much I know:

No fucking man will win my heart
Without stirring what's down below.

And once again,
Let me be blunt.
It's no longer my cunt.

Come in and sit.
Let's chat a bit,
And pretend we don't feel this need.

This driving desire,
The maddening fire,
This consumption of sexual greed.

My body reacts
To your torrid attacks,
And I crave your lustful touch.

You from behind
Is scorched in my mind,
And I've never **wanted** so much.

I pool my defenses,
Losing my senses,
And shove you outside my door.

My will almost shatters,
The experience matters,
And I have never wanted you more.

Compel me—
Words or action.
Surprise me.

I'm often not surprised anymore.
Unless at myself
By my own hand.

Fight with me.
I need signs of life.
Intelligent life is even better.

Seduce me.
If you dare.
I'm one tough cookie
But when there . . .

Compel me.

Does anyone out there hear me?
Or is it the same song
Sung by myself
To myself?
Sing a song of sad chick,
Pocket full of guys . . .
Five-and-twenty suicides
Packed in a night.
Some will rise.
Some will fall.
Dash away,
Dash away,
Run them all off.

Never let me stop and think,
Keep the world turning.
Stopping makes the pain grow strong
And feeds my insatiable yearning.

He takes me to places
Other men can only hope to go,
Dream to go,
Long to go.

He flatters me
With fingertips,
Tongue flicks,
And a fabulous prick.

. . . But it's deeper than that.

With him,
I am never at ease,
Down on my knees,
Submitting to him.

He dominates my thoughts
As much as my body.

Sinking deeper
Into my skin,

Again

And again,

Farther,

Within.

Strip down the frills,
The boisterous display,
The seduction,
And the mayhem
And animosity.

Strip down the fear
And moral decay,
Where my judgment
Supersedes where
My body does lay.

There,
Corpse inside,
Harbors my core
That men adore
And I abhor.

The wrenching pain
Of wanting
More.

The many ends
That I explore.

But in the center,
Buried inside,
Is a glowing nucleus
Of pure-hearted hope,
And a closeted romantic,
Neck dangling from rope.

Yes, I remember.

Fingers in my hair,
Flesh, pink and bare,
You always had flair
For discovery.

Yes, I surrendered.

Knelt at your feet,
Worshipped your meat,
Feigned the defeat
For ecstasy.

Yes, it still renders.

Images in my head,
Tears from the dread,
Choking words unsaid
For eternity.

She told herself no more.

No meaningless affairs.
No ruling heart over head.

She told herself to give up.

Lock up her heart
And never love another.

She told herself never give in.

No matter how he affected her.

Quiet confidence,
Bold outlook,
Comforting mystery.

She told herself . . .

But kiss him.

She never wore
The same disguise,
Except for her eyes,
Which gave her away
Far too easily.

She changed herself
As much as her shoes,
And this girl _liked_ shoes.

It was who she was,
How she was brought up,
And the experiences
She had acquired in life.

He was drugged by her.
She wasn't bound by
Limits of normal women.

She wasn't bound by
Anything.

And tonight,
She was fixated on him,
And he submitted amiably
To all the mystery.

I've made a habit
Of running from men,
Of remaining closed up,
Never letting them in.

I allowed the fear
To control my head,
To harvest the bounty
Where hope was fed.

A habit that you made
Easy to break.
A modified behavior
For betterment's sake.

Or perhaps substitution—
A vice for a vice.
Running now replaced
By a woman enticed.

I play with them
To prove to myself
That you have
No effect on me.

Elaborate schemes
Of bondage
And decorum.

I dangle the sex
On the end of a stick,
And watch them
Chase themselves madly.

It makes me
Not miss you
So badly.

But every once in a while
On a night like this,
I find a place
To somehow wish
I were anywhere
Near you.

I lay down tonight,
Unable to sleep.
Haunted by your absence.
Body feverishly
Tossing,
Trying to expel the thought of you
So that I might have
Momentary relief.

I long to feel your hands,
Your tongue,
Your cock . . .
Over me
And inside me.

I long to get sucked
Into your brain.
Learn all that you know.
How
And Why
You see the world
As you do.

I want to consume you
And be consumed by you.

I want the physical
And the metaphysical.

Give it to me.

I just want to be in this moment,
Hold onto this feather dream
A few more hours.

I want to hold your hand,
Suck your cock,
And write about it afterward.

I get lost in you
And lose you
Somewhere inside me.

I get found in you
And find you
Along the way.

I part my thighs
Ocean wide
And give into the tide.
The pulsing wave
That washes over
And strips me of my pride.
Desire and ache
So seeded within,
They wash me into shore—
A place so dry
It leaves me there
Always wanting
More.

Get to the
Cock—
Drop,
And roll . . .
Your tongue
Over and around it,
Upside and down it.

Demanding your full attention.

Instantly feel the expansion.
Power becomes commanding,
And every flick
Is torturous touch.

It now threatens to bust.

I trace the bulging veins
Of stiffened staff
With a vodka-soaked tongue
And a joint and a half.

I tease the head
With soft lips
And a fiendish grin.
I literally taste the sin.

Just a drop . . . again . . .

I take it in
And tighten my lips,
Starting in my hips,
I wave upon you
Slowly
Working

My
Way
D
o
w
n . . .

The only sound
Is your
Breathing.

Quick,
HEAVY
Breaths
Of wanting
To Be Taken
Over the
Edge
Of Release . . .

On all fours, I retract
Slowly
Working
My way
K . . .
C
A
B

This moment
You extract—

. . . And I drink in your essence
And my ego.

#1

He moves me in directions
Through planes of existence
Mortal men could never hope to comprehend.
He teaches me existentialism
By merely being
And wraps me in sensual suspension
Levitating above myself and my morals.
There's a sickness seeded deep inside
That draws me to him,
A twisted magnetism and weakened defense
That makes me uneasy.
I try to fight,
To deny,
To ignore,
But I end up wanting more.
He's in my fantasies.
He's in my nightmares.
He's in my head.
And apparently,
There's nothing I can do
To stop it.

#2

Mystery Maker,
Heart Breaker,
Devil in sheep's clothing.
Dominator,
Demonstrator,
Categorical phenomenon.
Manipulator,
Gullible crusader,
Boy behind the man.
Unknowing victim,
Knowing victim,
He knows who I am.

Eight dozen flashes
Stand for reasons why—

Why I should hate you,
Why I should rape you,
Why I should listen . . .

But I'm in no position
To fight it.

Truth be told,
I like it.

I crave it
Like I crave
You.

You—

The object of my desire,
The source of my fire.

Yeah, you're a liar,
But you do it elegantly . . .

Almost perfectly,
Which is why I stay.

We both know that at any time,
I could walk away,
But I <u>do</u> stay.

Part of me
Is waiting to see
The outcome of it.

I'm interested
In the games that we play,
The go-and-then-stay,
The push-and-pull away,
Our graphic display
Of something so powerful,
The-harder-you-try-not-to-think,
The-more-you-can't-help-but
Scenario.

That's what keeps me here.

I'm waiting
Until you see
It's always been me

And give in
To the power of
We.

Inside my head,
Where fantasy is fed,
You never buck
Against my current.

You're in the moment,
Willing suspension
Of belief.

It's a relief.

. . . To be able
To let my guard down.

I save a side
Of me
For you
That no one gets to see.

And I make you believe
I am
Everything
You ever wanted me
To be.

Let's stay here
In fantasy.

Fifty times I scold myself.
I want to shed my skin
And chew my flesh
For continuing to let you in.

Can it be I hate myself
So much that I submit
To the fuck in your fingertips
And the babble of bullshit?

You feign emotional connection,
And I try to play along.

Your sharp tongue twists the words
Into truths both strong
And wrong.

Intoxicated, I close my eyes
Where ecstasy comes in waves.
Fingertips followed by lips
Where resistance is concave.

My desire for desire's sake
Propels me to express
My skin and liquid cock dance,
Each moment I confess.

Then, comes the gush
Of selfish lust,
And other carnal things.
I can feel the retraction
That climax always brings.

The emotion makes you uneasy
As much as it finds me.
Dressing while you're pulling out,
You sigh,
Excuse,
Then leave.

It's become a familiar dance
Of a playboy and desperate whore.

The costumes we don,
And the roles we explore.

Can it be I hate myself
So much that I ignore,

The pathetic whorish thought
That I don't deserve more?

A futile illusion
Turned delusion,
And yes
. . . He takes me there.

It's the scent of his skin,
The way I take him in,
The inspiration of sin.
. . . He takes me there.

It's the path of his curves,
His will that I serve,
The glory in his nerve.
. . . He takes me there.

It's the force that he takes,
My willpower he rapes,
My heart that he breaks.
. . . And he takes me there.

It's the point I become
Utterly unnumb
And start to become.
. . . He takes me there.

When eyes lock with eyes,
The truth becomes lies,
And neither of us deny.
. . . He takes me *there*.

Let your skeletons take him out!
I heard her shout.
I heard her shout.

The eclipse hangs high.
Strike without doubt.
Strike without doubt.

And the witch flew down,
Looked me deep in the eye,
And studied my face.

"The eclipse is high,"
She said as her finger
Came straight to my nose.
"In this world," she whispered,
"Anything goes."

"You must learn to expand
And contract with your soul.
I foresee a big hole.
Just so you know."

"What do you suggest?"
I inquired of her.
"Should I withdrawal in terror?
Or blaze forth in fury?"

"You must tiptoe out bravely
And remember to breathe.
He's only what you want.
He's not what you need."

Into me . . .
Into me . . .
Resistance won't curb
Where you want to be.

You opened the box,
My calamity,
And now must decide
If you want to believe.

Give me a sign
You truly see,
I'm more than
What I claim to be.

And somewhere
In that unity,
You'll find
It was always
You . . .
And me.

Into we . . .
Into we . . .